CHRIS

MW01274366

THOMAS
À KEMPIS

Imitating Jesus

6 studies
for individuals
or groups
with study notes

CLASSICS

Carolyn Nystrom

CAROLYN NYSTROM, Series Editor

InterVarsity Press
Downers Grove, Illinois

InterVarsity Press
P.O. Box 1400, Downers Grove, IL 60515-1426
World Wide Web: www.ivpress.com
E-mail: mail@ivpress.com

InterVarsity Press® *is the book-publishing division of InterVarsity Christian Fellowship/USA*®, *a student movement active on campus at hundreds of universities, colleges and schools of nursing in the United States of America, and a member movement of the International Fellowship of Evangelical Students. For information about local and regional activities, write Public Relations Dept., InterVarsity Christian Fellowship/USA, 6400 Schroeder Rd., P.O. Box 7895, Madison, WI 53707-7895, or visit the IVCF website at <www.ivcf.org>.*

All Scripture quotations, unless otherwise indicated, are taken from the Holy Bible, New International Version®. NIV®. *Copyright ©1973, 1978, 1984 by International Bible Society. Used by permission of Zondervan Publishing House. All rights reserved.*

Note: Several questions in study two are adapted from John Stott, The Message of the Sermon on the Mount *(Downers Grove, Ill.: InterVarsity Press, 1978).*

Richard Gillard's "Servant Song" ©1977 Scripture in Song (A div. of Integrity Music, Inc.)/ASCAP. All rights reserved. International copyright secured. Used by permission c/o Integrity Music, Inc., 1000 Cody Road, Mobile, AL 36695

Cover and interior illustrations: Roberta Polfus

ISBN 0-8308-2082-5

Printed in the United States of America ∞

P	17	16	15	14	13	12	11	10	9	8	7	6	5	4	3	2	1
Y	16	15	14	13	12	11	10	09	08	07	06	05	04	03	02		

CONTENTS

Introducing
Thomas à Kempis

For years a tattered yellowed paperback lay among the clutter on my husband's bedside table. Eventually the pages became ragged and torn at the edges, some falling loose as I dusted. I would pick it up, read a snatched paragraph here and there, and return to my cleaning. I recognized the title and the author (both important), and on less busy days I sat down with the now-mangy book and tried to do some serious reading. I found in this book by Thomas à Kempis an intense devotion to Christ and a challenging call to discipleship. But it seemed . . . well, . . . hard. And unfamiliar. I quickly returned to the well-thumbed pages and familiar phrases of my NIV. At least *these* words were inspired by God.

A graduate class in medieval theology, taught by a monastic oblate, broadened my tastes. I learned that faithful monks had preserved Christianity through a thousand years of illiteracy, poverty and political unrest. They knew the Scripture and copied it painstakingly letter by letter. They served their communities with the compassion of Christ as they cared for the poor, the sick and the orphaned. And for much of that time, the best (and often only) education came from the monasteries. True, medieval monks were not without fault. Some were cruel, stupid, lecherous and hypocritical. But a parent of that era wanting her child to grow up in a safe environment with kind discipline, a fine education and a thorough grounding in the Christian faith both lived and taught, might well think of a monastery. As for career options, the monastic life offered constant work, few worries about food, income or lodging, and lifelong spiritual preparation for eternity with God.

A Religious Beginning

So it was that in 1392, twelve-year-old Thomas Haemerken arrived on the doorstep of Florentius Radewijns in the town of Deventer in what is now the Netherlands. He had traveled some fifty miles north from his home in the German town of Kempen located fifteen miles northeast of what is now Düsseldorf. Thomas was to follow his older brother John into "The Brotherhood of the Common Life." It was a momentous decision for the young man—impacting some six hundred years of Christians to follow.

Thomas had been born in 1379 or 1380 to John and Gertrude Haemerken. As was common at that time, the last name designated occupation—which might explain why Thomas did not retain it. Haemerken means "hammer," so his father was probably a blacksmith. Thomas would later be known by the name à Kempis, meaning simply "from the town of Kempen." His mother taught a school for small children, where Thomas probably began his education.

School usually began for boys at about the age of seven. It might be a "reading school" emphasizing written words or a "song school" where much of the learning came through music. A reading school taught students to read the local language. For Thomas, this was an early form of German. And since Latin was the universal language of the church, even young boys were expected to begin acquiring this important tool that would allow them eventually to communicate with Christian scholars throughout the world. A song school taught hymns (both tunes and words) and principles of the Christian faith—sung. Both forms of school taught arithmetic, prayers and basic writing, with a strong emphasis on tending to the spiritual needs of the boys in their care.

In between the ages of twelve and fourteen, a boy was expected to make some serious choices. He would choose a future occupation and begin to work, or enter a school to prepare for that work. He would also become engaged or affirm a prior engagement made by his parents—unless, of course, the boy was headed for the church. It appears that Thomas (or his parents) chose the church.

Life in the Monastery
The Brotherhood of the Common Life, which Thomas entered at age twelve, was a loosely formed organization created by Gerard Groote, in about 1374, for the purpose of living as closely as possible in the style of the early Christians. People in the brotherhood (and eventually sisterhood) were not necessarily monks and nuns. They might live in their own homes, or they might share a common house. But they held their goods in common, and they devoted themselves to prayer, the moral teachings of Jesus and caring for the poor—especially children. People of the Common Life worked, often as copyists, creating many of the beautifully illustrated manuscripts of the late Middle Ages. But in keeping with their principle of charity, each copyist would spend at least one hour, twice a week, writing for the poor.

These men and women of the Common Life earned a reputation for intense devotion to Christ, even at great personal cost. Groote himself went to care for a dying friend, a task most people refused in an era ravaged by the plague. In spite of his care, the friend died. A few days later, so did Gerard Groote at the age of forty-four—leaving the Common Life ministry only ten years established. But it grew. By 1400, a hundred houses for Brothers of the Common Life dotted northern Europe—and three hundred for Sisters of the Common Life. Their devotion to Christ created a whole movement termed *devotio moderna* or "modern devotion." The original house of the Brotherhood was in Deventer under the charge of Florentius Radewijns. It was this home that the young Thomas à Kempis entered in 1392 at the age of twelve.

But Groote himself had expected that a loose organization of laypeople connected only by common goods, works of charity and holy living might not provide enough structure for those seeking extended times of prayer apart from the temptations of ordinary life. So he suggested the alternative of a monastery and even picked out a site at Windesheim—some twelve miles north of Deventer just outside the town of Zwolle. In fact, by the time Thomas arrived at Deventer, his brother John (fifteen years older than he) was already one of the six founding leaders at Mount St. Agnes, a second nearby monastery under Windesheim's care. Thomas would eventually join John there as an Augustinian monk taking vows of poverty, chastity and obedience in about 1406 around the age of twenty-six. Later, at the age of thirty-three, Thomas took ordination vows as a priest and then remained at St. Agnes (except for a three-year exile) until the end of his long life in 1471. John, on the other hand, was soon sent in by the Chapter of Windesheim to start a new community in 1408 at Bommel on the Rhine.

What was it like to live the life of an Augustinian monk in the 1400s? Much of life revolved within the enclosure of the monastery. Monks would go for years, if not decades, and never leave its walls. Its regular cycle of devotion called the monks to chapel and to prayer seven times in twenty-four hours—including one service at 2:00 a.m. They memorized the psalms and sang them through (all one hundred fifty) each week. Many monks were copyists, and this itself was a spiritual discipline. An old rule admonished them to "attend in your copying to three things, to wit, that you make the letters properly and perfectly, that you copy without error; and that you understand the sense of what you are copying; and that you concentrate your wandering mind on the task." But not all of the monks worked at copying (though Thomas à Kempis did). Other monks worked as gardeners, builders, preachers and (because of the many impoverished children in their care) teachers. But everyone worked.

As for behavior, all of life was to be guided by Christ's command of love toward God and toward other people. This encompassed body, mind and soul. For the body, monks were to practice simplicity in dress, food, drink and work. For the mind, they were to practice humble love toward all—especially the young, the sick and the sinful. For the soul, they were to love God unselfishly, not for what they could know of him or what they could gain from him but for who he is. And they were to live every moment in an attitude of prayer. With seven cycles a day, prayer reminders came frequently.

Augustinian monks drew their name from the great theologian Augustine of Hippo (354-430), and they followed his teachings about monastic life. But though Augustine was a scholar, not many Augustinians of the fourteenth century cut fresh theological ground. Instead they focused on devotion to Christ and living out, with a tender conscience, the theological principles they already knew. Thomas à Kempis wrote, "I had rather feel compunction of heart for my sins than only know the definition of compunction." As for the necessary restrictions of life inside monastic walls, Thomas seemed content. He wrote, "I sought for rest but never found it, save in a little corner with a little book."

Life Outside the Monastery
Meanwhile, life outside monastic walls was far from peaceful in the late Middle Ages. War had raged so long between England and France that it became known as The Hundred Years' War. In fact, these countries battled intermittently even longer—from 1337 to 1453, each claiming sections of the other's territory depending on which monarch ruled. The war itself extended within a hundred miles of the St. Agnes monastery, though resulting unrest shook all of Europe throughout that time. In 1453 the war stumbled to an end without even the formality of a truce. Contemporary borders emerged, except that England still claimed Calais—which she surrendered in 1558. Thomas à Kempis lived through this war all of his life—up until he was seventy-three years old.

Church wars were even worse. In 1309, the church became so unwelcome in southern Italy that the pope left Rome and took up residence in Avignon in what would later become France. This "Babylonian Captivity" lasted until 1377. The next year, the church tried to return her pope to Rome, but the election got so unruly that two popes emerged and neither would give way to the other. As if that were not divisive enough, thirty-seven years later (in 1409) a third pope was elected in the Italian city of Pisa. Clearly something had to be done or the church would fragment in all directions. So from 1414 to 1418, three hundred bishops, twenty-nine cardinals, three patriarchs, thirty-three archbishops, and a host of abbots and doctors of theology met at the Council of Constance to try to solve the problem. After three years they were able to rid themselves of the three popes and elect a single pope (Martin IV) to head the church, which by that time had endured a splintered papacy for thirty-nine years. At the age of thirty-seven, Thomas à Kempis had lived his entire life to that point under divided authority at the top of his church.

Disease decimated Europe. In 1347 a war vessel from Asia docked in a Mediterranean port—and death swept through Europe for the next three years, finally arriving in the Low Countries in 1349. A person would become ill, lymph nodes swelling to orange-sized *boubons*. Seventy percent of them would be dead in six days—some within hours. Twenty percent would develop the disease in their lungs, a pneumonic variety of the plague. These would always die, but first each cough and sneeze would further spread the disease. One third of Europe died in the first round of the plague.

During the next fifty years the plague made a reappearance each decade, stacking up more deaths. Monasteries, with their enclosed living arrangements (and their willingness to care for the sick), were especially hard hit. In 1400, England contained a mere half of the population she had held one hundred years prior, and a thousand English villages were void of living humans. Throughout Europe fields returned to forests with no one to till the soil. We now know that flea-infected rats brought the disease and that today's antibiotics can cure it. But this "Black Death" was a mystery to people of the late Middle Ages. Many saw this raging death connected to God in some way, but what kind of God? When Thomas à Kempis took his monastic vows at the age of twenty-six, he had lived in the shadow of bubonic plague all of his life.

A reformation brewed—but hadn't yet begun. John Wycliffe (1329/30-1384) lived and taught in England. He believed that Scriptures ought to be in the hands of the people and so translated the Bible into English and encouraged them to read it. He questioned the doctrine of transubstantiation, suggesting that the elements of communion remained literal bread and wine—that only in a figurative and sacramental sense did they become the body and blood of Christ. He believed that people were redeemed through the sacrament, but only if they received it with a repentant attitude. He thought that preaching the Scripture was a sacrament equal to communion. He questioned the authority of the pope (popes) and of the priests, saying that if they did not live a godly life they had no authority, and that no human priest could mediate between God and people. He said that monasteries ought to be closed and their goods distributed to the people. For these heresies, Wycliffe's followers were dubbed "lollards," meaning mumblers or idlers. In 1384, Wycliffe died suddenly of "apoplexy" to the great relief of Catholic authorities. But four hundred years later Protestants would claim him and honor his name in a host of Bible translations created for people who would not otherwise have Scriptures in their own language. Thomas à Kempis was four years old at Wycliffe's death.

John Hus (1372?-1415) followed in the steps of Wycliffe, but from the far distance of Czech. Hus believed that a bishop was a true officer of the church only if he lived a godly life. He believed that the real church was eternal and many people in the current earthly church were not in that eternal church. He believed that God predestined some people to come to faith in him and that these people would live obviously godly lives. And he believed that a pope was a pope only to the extent that his conduct marked him as a disciple of Jesus. The Council of Constance, meeting to resolve the problem of three simultaneous popes, had little patience with John Hus. They invited him there with a guarantee of "safe conduct," then tried him for heresy and burned him at the stake. Hus died pardoning his accusers and reciting the Creed.

Thomas à Kempis was thirty-five at the time.

If Thomas had known them, he would not have approved of Hus or Wycliffe. They were forerunners of a coming Protestant Reformation. Thomas à Kempis was and would always remain a Catholic, loyal to the doctrines of the church and to the authority of the pope. But millions of Protestants, long after Thomas was dead, would read and grow toward Christ through his work.

Thomas à Kempis and His (?) Book

For most Christians, Thomas à Kempis is known for one thing and one thing only: *The Imitation of Christ.* The book went through eighteen hundred printings by the eighteenth century, is available in more than a hundred languages today and has been read by over a billion people. It has been termed "the second-best selling religious book of all time"—second, of course, to the Bible.

The Imitation of Christ was written in the early fifteenth century by a monk for monks. So it is a mistake to assume that we can pull each sentence into our twenty-first-century living rooms and put it to work. But given that reminder, today's Christian will find a gracious invitation to follow the path that Jesus has walked ahead of us. The book is composed of four parts. Book one speaks of basic principles of the spiritual life. The opening paragraph sets the goal to "follow Christ" and to "conform our life as nearly as we can to his." Book two describes the inner life of a spiritually minded Christian. It speaks of humility, a pure conscience and friendship with Jesus. Book three is a dialogue with Christ, inviting us to prayer and to listening to what Jesus might say in response. Book four describes the sacrament of communion and how we can prepare to receive it. Far from extrabiblical, *Imitation* refers to more than a thousand biblical quotations. Clearly the author had soaked his mind in the written Word of God.

But who was that person, or persons? Thomas à Kempis was a copyist in a monastery full of copyists. Most of their manuscripts were unsigned—as are the earliest forms of *Imitation*. Sections of the book appeared as early as 1418. In 1434 a presentation copy merely said of the author, "He did not wish to name himself, and that will win him an eternal recompense; but Jesus knows him well." A later manuscript shows a signature with the words, "Finished and completed in the year of our Lord 1441 by the hand of Brother Thomas à Kempis, at Mount St. Agnes, near Zwolle." But was Thomas signing as an author or as a copyist? This manuscript is an obvious copy of an earlier work. His own?

Scholars have debated this mystery over the past five hundred years. Suggested authors include St. Bernard, St. Bonaventure, Ludolf of Saxony, John Gersen, Jean de Gerson, Gerard Grotte and (most frequently) Thomas à Kempis. It is almost certain that Thomas had *something* to do with the book. He may have compiled and copied earlier works of other authors adding his own touches as he went along. Or, it is entirely possible that he wrote the whole thing himself drawing on the principles taught throughout the Brotherhood of Common Life.

If Thomas à Kempis wrote all of *The Imitation of Christ,* it composes only one tenth of his full works. He also wrote a journal recording the events in his monastery, *The Chronicles of the Canons Regular of Mount St. Agnes.* He composed biographies of Gerald Groote and Florentius Radewijns (whose door he first entered at the age of twelve). *Soliloquy of the Soul* explores the yielding of our souls to the grace of God. He also wrote a variety of sermons, tracts and devotions. And beginning in 1425, he copied the entire Bible—in Latin. If assembled by today's presses, his written works would equal more than two thousand pages, not including the Latin Bible. But did he write *The Imitation of Christ?* We don't know. Does it matter? The writings it contains on the subject of personal humility would say, "Probably not." Perhaps the original inscription is most significant. God knows the author (or authors), and that is all that is important.

Our focus is on the book's goal: to show us how to imitate Christ. Jesus himself extends the invitation. "A student is not above his teacher, nor a servant above his master. It is enough for the student to be like his teacher and the servant like his master" (Matthew

10:24-25). A fourteenth-century monk, who spent his life writing and copying holy words, can lead us into following Jesus—his Lord and ours.

Translation Note

Excerpts from *The Imitation of Christ* come from the Knox-Oakley translation. Monsignor R. A. Knox, a British Latin scholar, translated the New Testament from the Latin Vulgate into English, finishing that work in 1949. He then began work on *Imitation* using his thumb-worn copy (given to him at his ordination into the priesthood), smoothing the Latin text into straightforward English. "If I die without finishing my translation of *The Imitation of Christ,* please tell my executors from me that you are to finish it," he wrote to his young friend Michael Oakley.

After a lifetime of living with the book, Monsignor Knox recognized its challenges. "If a man tells you that he is fond of the *Imitation,* view him with sudden suspicion; he is either a dabbler or a saint." By 1957 when Knox was well into the painstaking work, he knew that his time was short. So he again wrote to Oakley, "I'm afraid that the present state of my health makes it unlikely that I shall go on with it. . . . My idea has been to get rid of the theological terms (which Thomas à Kempis uses rather uncomprehendingly, I think) . . . i.e., I wanted to turn it into a human document." Two months later Knox was dead, and friends handed to Oakley the tattered Latin original that had been Knox's guide. Michael Oakley picked up his work at book two, chapter four, where Knox had left off. The resulting unpretentious English is what we now have.

But we must not let the simple language mislead us. Knox warns us from his own lifelong experience: "The whole work was meant to be, surely what it is—sustained irritant which will preserve us, if it is read faithfully, from sinking back into relaxation: from self-conceit, self-pity, self-love. It offers consolation here and there, but always at the price of fresh exertion, of keeping your head pointing upstream. Heaven help us if we find easy reading in *The Imitation of Christ.*"

How to Use a Christian Classics Bible Study

Christian Classics Bible studies are designed to introduce some of the key writers, preachers and teachers who have shaped our Christian thought over the centuries. Each guide has an introduction to the life and thought of a particular writer and six study sessions. The studies each have an introduction to the particular themes and writings in that study and the following components.

READ ─────────────────────────────────────
This is an excerpt from the original writings.

GROUP DISCUSSION OR PERSONAL REFLECTION ────────
These questions are designed to help you explore the themes of the reading.

INTO THE WORD ───────────────────────────
This includes a key Scripture to read and explore inductively. The text picks up on the themes of the study session.

ALONG THE ROAD ──────────────────────────
These are ideas to carry you further and deeper into the themes of the study. Some can be used in a group session; many are for personal use and reflection.

The study notes at the end of the guide offer further helps and background on the study questions.

May these writings and studies enrich your life in Christ.

1

FOLLOWING JESUS

Matthew 4:18-22; 8:18-27

*F*ollowing Jesus is a lifetime commitment. For me that process began when, as a nine-year-old girl, I responded to the invitation of a revival preacher, knelt at the front of a small rural church and asked Jesus into my heart. But Jesus' call to follow him probably came long before that—voiced in the prayers and teachings of my parents almost from my birth. And it continued as Jesus called me to follow him through high school years when I felt isolated from other teens, through college years when I grew in quantum leaps of knowledge and faith. Jesus' call went on through young adult years when I turned aside from any serious form of discipleship, through the next stage as a foster parent to abused children when I learned that I had to trust God for their future, and through experiences of growing as a disciple of Jesus, able to disciple others. Jesus' calling continued through grief and the humility of depending on the faith of others in order to maintain my own, and it continued through the joy of studying the ancient fathers and mothers of the faith, seeing that they had walked the path of imitating Christ—long before my own unsteady steps.

Following Jesus is a lifelong process. As we grow and develop as people we become more complex beings. So we add each new complexity of what we have become into our commitment to Christ. And Christ continues to transform us into what he has designed us to become—people created in his image, damaged by our own sinful nature to be sure, but redeemed by his love and gradually being transformed into his likeness. Scripture points the way; we have the model of Jesus' life and teachings.

 WALKING IN LIGHT

THE IMITATION OF CHRIST 2.1, 2.11, 3.6

He who follows me can never walk in darkness, our Lord says. Here are words of Christ, words of warning; if we want to see our way truly, never a trace of blindness left in our hearts, it is his life, his character, we must take for our model. Clearly, then, we must make it our chief business to train our thoughts upon the life of Jesus Christ.

Christ's teaching—how it overshadows all the saints have to teach us! Could we but master its spirit, what a story of hidden manna we should find there! How is it that so many of us can hear the Gospel read out again and again, with so little emotion? Because they haven't got the Spirit of Christ; that is why. If a man wants to understand Christ's words fully, and relish the flavor of them, he must be one who is trying to fashion his whole life on Christ's model. . . .

Jesus today has many who love his heavenly kingdom, but few who carry his cross; many who yearn for comfort, few who long for distress. Plenty of people he finds to share his banquet, few to share his fast. Every one desires to take part in his rejoicing, but few are willing to suffer anything for his sake. There are many that follow Jesus as far as the breaking of bread, few as far as drinking the cup of suffering; many that revere his miracles, few that follow him in the indignity of his cross; many that love Jesus as long as nothing runs counter to them; many that praise and bless him, as long as they receive some comfort from him; but should Jesus hide from them and leave them for a while, they fall to complaining or become deeply depressed.

Those who love Jesus for his own sake, not for the sake of their own comfort, bless him in time of trouble and heartache as much as when they are full of consolation. . . .

Because the moment you come to the slightest obstacle you give up what you have begun and seek for comfort with the utmost eagerness. The brave lover stands fast in temptation, gives no credit to the subtle suggestions of his enemy the Devil. When things go well with him, I am his delight; so am I still when he meets with trouble.

An experienced lover heeds not so much the gift of the lover as the love of him that gave it. What he looks for is affection, not money; his Beloved is higher in his eyes than any gift. A noble lover does not rest content with a gift; he desires me rather than any gift I can make him. All is not lost, therefore, if you sometimes feel less love for me or my saints than you would like to. That good, sweet feeling you are aware of now and then is brought about by my grace working in you at that time; a kind of foretaste of your heavenly home. You must not depend too much upon it, though; it is a thing that comes and goes. What *is* a sure sign of virtue and of great merit is to fight against evil stirrings of the mind when they arise and to treat with contempt the suggestions of the Devil. . . .

The Lord is my light and my deliverance; whom have I to fear? Though a whole host were arrayed against me, my heart would be undaunted. God is our refuge and stronghold.

 GROUP DISCUSSION OR PERSONAL REFLECTION ——

1. *The Imitation of Christ* is a title that challenges all serious Christians. What do you know of Jesus that you would like to imitate? (In response to this question, Thomas à Kempis invites us to "train our thoughts upon the life of Christ.")

2. "Jesus today has many who love his heavenly kingdom, but few who bear his cross," writes Thomas à Kempis in paragraph three above. Study the six pairs of that paragraph—each suggesting a following by many and a following by few. To what extent would you like to be among the few?

What changes would it take in yourself to be in that company?

3. "An experienced lover heeds not so much the gift of the lover as the love of him that gave it," writes Thomas à Kempis. If you agree with this, how will it impact the way you follow Jesus?

INTO THE WORD ——————————————————

4. *Read Matthew 4:18-22 and 8:18-27.* Focus on the Matthew 4 passage. Place yourself in the scene as one of the four fishermen. What do you find compelling about this event?

5. As one of the fisherman, what would you be considering as you make your decision?

6. Focus on Matthew 8:19-22. In view of Jesus' conversation with these two people, what all does it mean to follow Jesus?

7. Why do you think Jesus made following him so demanding?

8. What has been difficult for you to give up in your discipleship to Jesus?

9. Focus on verses 23-27. What were the challenges of those following Jesus in this scene?

10. In verse 27 the disciples ask, "What kind of man is this?" How do the events surrounding the storm help to answer that question?

11. What have you learned about Jesus that encourages you to follow him?

12. Imitating Jesus is an impossible challenge, one that we can only fully meet when we are with him in eternity. What would you say to someone considering that journey who asks you, "Why should I follow Jesus?"

 ALONG THE ROAD ─────────────────────

What have been some of your steps in following Jesus? When and how did he call you to follow him? What decisions did you need to make along the way? What events or people has he used to increase your faith? Create a timeline marking these significant points. Pray, talking to God about what is revealed there.

Thomas à Kempis tells us that one of the challenges of following Jesus is to do so out of love for him—not merely because of whatever gifts that relationship might bring. How does the temptation to follow Jesus for "what I can get out of it" reveal itself in the way you pray?

in your association with other Christians?

in your obedience (or lack of obedience) to his commands?

❷ Good praying takes many forms, but in practice many of us focus on making requests of God—for ourselves or for others. Try to write a prayer that asks of God nothing at all. What does this exercise teach you about God?

about yourself?

❷ To the extent that you are able to do so with honesty, pray the prayer of Thomas à Kempis below. Pause at appropriate places to add your personal words of commitment.

FROM THE PRAYERS OF THOMAS À KEMPIS
The Imitation of Christ 4.16

O *sweetest and most loving Lord, . . . see, here I stand before you, naked and poor, begging for grace and imploring your pity. I am a beggar, and hungry; give me food. I am cold; warm me with the fire of your love. I am blind; enlighten my eyes with the brightness of your presence. Make all things on earth bitter to me, turn all affliction and trouble to patient acceptance; make me despise and forget all things below you, all things created. Lift up my heart to you in heaven; do not let me go, to be a wanderer over the face of the earth. Be my only delight, from now and for ever; you alone are my meat and my drink, my love and my joy, my sweetness, my all-embracing good.*

II

THE PATH OF GRACE
Matthew 5:1-12

*B*lessed are the meek, for they will inherit the earth." Jesus' advice in the Sermon on the Mount is *not* the key to success, at least not on this earth.

Robert W. Harvey, my pastor for most of my adult life, was meek. Bob had many pastoral skills, but he led the church not so much by skill as by character. In a church peopled by Ph.D.'s, he held a lowly M.Div. degree, but no one seemed to mind—least of all him. When he needed help with a Hebrew text, he simply consulted a resident expert, then led the congregation to live up to the teachings of the Scriptures before them.

Early in his ministry a music professor in our congregation noticed that Bob's ability to lead music was, well, meager. "Bob, you could use some help selecting hymns," he said. "I'd be glad to take that on." Bob (tone deaf) agreed with a grin, and that was the end of it. Bob stood behind the pulpit, microphone carefully turned off, and mouthed the words about a half-beat behind.

Administration wasn't his strong suit either. So instead of chairing our board (which was his right) he turned that over to an elder and simply sat at the table with the rest of us. On the rare occasions when he offered an opinion, we listened—carefully.

On Sunday morning, when our liturgy turned to confession, Bob led us, not by telling us what we ought to confess, but by gently confessing his own areas of sin—and inviting us to do the same.

This meek person was a powerful leader, pointing our whole congregation toward godliness—by his character. Here is an excerpt from a memorial tribute:

> Bob was a gentle shepherd. He wasn't like a cattle herder going out with lassos and spurs, but like a shepherd climbing rocky cliffs, in the dark, in the rain, at night, and drawing people—not to himself, but to God.
>
> He simply refused all temptations to power and chose instead to serve—and taught us to do the same. Our people run their businesses and classrooms and families differently because of Bob's model of living the life of a servant. In my own current work, when I am faced with a decision (in my best moments) I ask, not, "How can I win?" but "How can I better serve these people?" That is part of Bob's legacy to me, to the church.

"Blessed are the meek," said Jesus. But only God can turn our natural prideful nature into meekness. Thomas à Kempis wrote of this tension between our natural bent and a life modeled after Jesus. He called it "nature" and "grace."

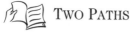 TWO PATHS ────────────────

THE IMITATION OF CHRIST 3.54

You must carefully notice the ways in which nature moves, and grace; these two ways are completely opposed, but so fine and hidden as hardly to be told apart. . . . Nature is crafty, many are those she betrays, ensnaring and deceiving them, ever having her own ends in view; grace makes her way unaffectedly, turning aside from anything that looks evil. She tries no trickery, but does everything simply for the sake of God, in whom she rests, making him the end of whatever she does. . . .

Nature works to advance her own interests, waiting to see how much gain will be coming to her from others. Grace, on the other hand, does not consider what may be of profit or advantage to herself, but what may benefit many.

Nature is glad to receive honor and respect; grace faithfully ascribed all honor and glory to God.

Nature is afraid of disgrace and scorn; grace is glad to suffer shame for the name of Jesus.

Nature loves taking it easy, loves giving the body rest; grace cannot be unoccupied, but is glad to take up some work.

Nature collects rare and beautiful things and disdains what is coarse and cheap; grace is pleased with simple, humble things, does not look askance at what is rough or jibe at dressing in old rags.

Nature has her eye on worldly matters, is cheered by material gain and grieved by its loss, and is stung to anger by the least unkind remark; but grace is concerned with what is eternal, is not attached to the things of time. The loss of her goods does not worry her, nor is she embittered by the harsh comments of others, because she has placed her treasure and her joy in heaven, where nothing is ever lost.

Nature is greedy; she would much rather receive than give, and holds on to her property with possessive love; grace is kind and unselfish, believes in sharing, is quite happy with little, and reckons that giving presents makes one happier than receiving them. . . .

Nature loves having a crowd of friends and relations, and takes pride in her stately family seat and her distinguished pedigree; she puts on her best smile for those who have influence, says nice things to those with money, and approves of those who share her attitude to life. Grace is different; she loves even her enemies, and does not boast of having a large number of friends. Stately homes and noble birth mean nothing to her, unless she finds greater holiness there. It is the poor she favors rather than the rich; simple, good people she has more in common with than with the influential; she likes those who say what they mean, not liars. She is always encouraging good people to aim at higher prizes, and by their virtues to grow more and more like the Son of God.

It is not long before nature starts grumbling when things are scarce or when trouble comes; grace endures poverty as long as it lasts.

Nature sees everything from her own selfish point of view; all her struggling and striving are for herself alone. Grace, on the other hand, refers everything to God, from whom it came in the beginning; she never attributes any good to herself or has the arrogance to presume it to be hers; she does not argue or put her own views before other people's, but in all that touches her senses and her understanding submits to the eternal wisdom and the judgment of God. . . .

She has no wish to advertise herself and her deeds, but her desire is that God may be blessed in his gifts, all of which he showers on men simply for love.

This grace is a supernatural light, a kind of special gift of God. It is the peculiar seal of those whom God has chosen, and a pledge of eternal salvation, lifting a man up from the things of earth to love the things of heaven, making a spiritual man of a worldling. You see, then, that the more nature is kept down and overcome, the greater is the grace that floods a man's soul; and every day, as fresh streams of grace come to him, his inner self is being remolded, until he takes on the likeness of God.

 GROUP DISCUSSION OR PERSONAL REFLECTION ⸺

1. What is your overall impression of Thomas's description of nature and grace?

2. Create a visual display so that you can clearly see the contrast Thomas à Kempis draws between people guided by human nature and people guided by God's grace. (Use two different highlighters to mark the text, or list the qualities in two labeled columns, or mark each description in the text with an N or a G.) How would the culture in which you live view these two lists?

3. What do you find particularly challenging about a life of grace as Thomas à Kempis describes it?

 INTO THE WORD————————————————————

4. *Read Matthew 5:1-12.* What would the disciples find startling about Jesus' description of people who are blessed?

5. To be "poor in spirit" (v. 3) is to know our spiritual bankruptcy before God. Why is this essential to entering the kingdom of heaven?

6. Mourning (v. 4) might come from grief or personal loss, and this is one of the forms of mourning that Jesus blesses. But mourning might also come from a sorrow over sin—our own sin or the sin of a group to which we belong, for example our church, our segment of society or our nation. What causes you to mourn?

7. People who are meek (v. 5) are able to see themselves with honest humility and therefore cultivate a gentle attitude toward others. Who have you known to exhibit these qualities?

8. Focus on verse 6 and spend a few moments thinking about the words "hunger," "thirst" and "righteousness." What personal hope do you find in Jesus' promise here?

9. Why do you think Jesus links the mercy we show to others with God's mercy to us (v. 7)?

10. What does it mean to be pure of heart toward God?

toward people (v. 8)?

11. Consider verse 9. What opportunities do you have to make peace in your family, church, work or community?

12. What warnings and what encouragement do you find in verses 10-12?

13. People who live by what Thomas à Kempis called "grace" live differently than the rest of the world, but Jesus called them "blessed." In spite of the challenges, why might you choose to walk this path?

 ALONG THE ROAD ————————————————

⌇ Slowly reread Thomas's writing, contrasting nature and grace. As you consider each set of contrasts, put your initial next to what best describes you. Bring to God in prayer what this reveals about yourself. If you are able, prayerfully set a goal of one area in which you will move away from following human nature and toward following the nature of God's grace.

Reread the Beatitudes of Matthew 5:1-12. List the "blesseds" and next to each write the name of someone you know who exemplifies that quality. Thank God for these people and for the promised blessing that God offers to each one.

Select one of the Beatitudes of Matthew 5 and focus on it for one week, looking for opportunities to live out this quality. Make journal notes of your successes and also of your missed opportunities. At the close of your journal entries, write the statement of blessing from that particular Beatitude, remembering that it is Jesus' prayer for you.

FROM THE PRAYERS OF THOMAS À KEMPIS

The Imitation of Christ 3.55

The Learner: O Lord my God, you have made me in your own image and likeness; grant me this grace, which, as you have shown, is so great a one, so necessary if I am to be saved: the grace of overcoming my own evil propensities, which drag me into sin and the loss of my soul. I am aware in my body of the authority of sin, opposing the authority of my mind, leading me away in bondage to give in to my sensual inclinations in many a way. I cannot resist its fierce promptings unless your holy grace comes to my rescue, filling my heart with its fiery glow.

III

THE PATH OF HUMILITY
John 13:1-17

*I*t was the evening of Maundy Thursday. Dim lights softened the corners of our church sanctuary. White-draped communion tables waited in the center aisle. We would remember together the last meal Jesus ate with his disciples, a holy, intimate time in which Jesus instituted the eucharistic sacrament. We suburban Presbyterians would use our accustomed Scottish form of communion where we sit at tables and receive the bread and the cup. Over and over I would say, eye to eye, to those seated before me, "Jim (or Sue or Mario), this is the body of Christ broken for you." And later, with the cup, "This cup is the new covenant of Christ's blood shed for you." It is a holy time, one mingled with song and prayer and tears of thanksgiving. Christ meets us there, leveling the differences among us as we partake together of his grace.

But this year, after the sermon and communion, we would do something new—for us. We would also remind ourselves of what Jesus did at the close of that first communion meal. Standing stark in the chancel lights at the front of the church stood four empty chairs, each surrounded by water pitchers and mismatched towels. Jesus washed feet that last night with his disciples—and we would do the same. Washing feet in a public worship service is a stretch; most of us prefer to wash our own feet—in private. So four of us would demonstrate before inviting others to join us. Barefoot, I walked to the front with another woman and knelt before a chair. As I gently poured water over one foot and into the waiting tub, I was conscious of her careful manicure (and my own bunions), which seemed to somehow represent the world of social difference between us. Yet as I poured, I could look up into her face and say, "I wash your feet in the name of Christ." And as I poured water over her other foot and then wiped it dry, I spoke, "As Christ has served us, let us serve each other." She did the same for me. Washing and being washed. Both are humbling—as Jesus intended.

Months later I would sit across a conference table from the same woman and take an opposite position from hers on what we both considered an important church issue. But we would remember our vows to serve each other on that Maundy Thursday. Even though we disagreed, we would honor those vows in our debate—and its aftermath.

 LIVING HUMBLE —————————————————————

THE IMITATION OF CHRIST 1.14, 3.8

Watch your own step; be slow to criticize the doings of other people. When we criticize others, we get nothing for our pains; how often we make mistakes! How carelessly it can lead us into sin! Be your own critic; pull yourself to pieces; then you will have something to show for your trouble. Again and again our judgment about a thing depends on the way our sympathies are engaged; a personal preference can easily rob us of the power to see straight. This obstinacy in our own opinions would have less power to disturb our judgments, if all the desire of our hearts found its only scope in God.

But too often some hidden force within, some attraction that meets us from the outside, will sweep us off our feet. Plenty of people are influenced in their actions by these undercurrents of self-seeking, without having any idea of it. All seems to go well with them, as long as everything turns out in accordance with their wishes, their plans; but when once their wills are thwarted, they lose their balance and get depressed in no time. . . .

The Learner: Dust and ashes though I be, I have taken it upon me to speak to my Lord. If I think anything more of myself than that, you stand on the opposite side of the court, while my sins give evidence, true evidence I cannot deny. But if I admit my insignificance, confess I am but nothing, turn away from all my self-importance and bring myself down to the level of the dust that I am, your grace will be merciful toward me, your light will be close to my heart; and all my self-esteem infinitesimal though it be, will be drowned in the abyss of my own nothingness and be for ever no more. That is the way you show me my real self—what I am, what I have been, what I have become; because I am nothing, and did not even know it. Left to myself, I am but nothing, a mere mass of weakness; the moment you look upon me, I at once become strong and filled with fresh joy. Your raising me so speedily, embracing me so tenderly, overwhelms me with amazement, seeing that the weight of my own sinfulness is always dragging me downward.

It is your love that brings this about, freely forestalling me and coming to my help in my countless needs, guarding me from grave dangers and snatching me away, as I am bound to confess, from evils past reckoning. It was through loving myself in the wrong way that I lost myself; by seeking you alone and loving you sincerely, I have found both myself and you. My love for you has made me shrivel even more completely into the nothingness that I am. You deal with me, my dearest love, far above what I deserve, far above anything I dare hope for or ask for.

My God, may you be blessed; for though I am unworthy of any kindness, yet your generosity, your limitless bounty, never ceases to do good even to those who are ungrateful, to those who have turned far away from you. Turn us back to you, that we may be

grateful, humble and devout; for you are our souls' health, our virtue, our strength.

 GROUP DISCUSSION OR PERSONAL REFLECTION

1. One way to learn humility is to know God. What do you see of
God in these five paragraphs from Thomas à Kempis?

2. What is dangerous about judging people—including ourselves
(see paragraphs one and two)?

3. What is the value of humility according to Thomas à Kempis
(see paragraphs three and four)?

4. In paragraph four Thomas says to God, "It was through loving
myself in the wrong way that I lost myself; by seeking you alone and

loving you sincerely, I have found both myself and you." What all do you think Thomas means by this statement?

 INTO THE WORD ⎯⎯⎯⎯⎯⎯⎯⎯⎯⎯⎯⎯⎯

5. *Read John 13:1-17.* As you read, place yourself in this scene as one of the characters. Who are you and what is your sense of what is happening here?

6. Verse 1 says that Jesus loved his own and "now showed them the full extent of his love." In what ways do you see the love of Jesus in this event?

7. Verse 3 begins, "Jesus knew." What all did Jesus know and how is that connected to what he did in verse 4?

8. What all took place in the dialogue between Jesus and Peter (vv. 6-11)?

9. What do you think would be hard about having Jesus wash your feet?

10. If you were painting a picture of Jesus washing the feet of Judas, what emotions would you try to capture (vv. 2, 11)?

11. Focus on verses 12-17. Thoughtfully read aloud verses 14-15. In practical terms, what does a humble attitude of washing another person's feet do to your relationship with that person?

12. Bring to mind a current relationship that is tense. What would it mean for you to wash that person's feet?

to allow that person to wash yours?

 ALONG THE ROAD ─────────────────────────

Jesus asked his disciples, "Do you understand what I have done for you?" Write your answer to this question in the form of a prayer to Jesus.

If you are meeting with a group, consider washing each other's feet in much the same way that Jesus did. You'll need a large tub, towels and a large pitcher of warm water. Remove your shoes and socks. One person sits on a chair holding a foot over the tub. The other kneels and pours water over the foot, letting the water run into the tub, and then wipes the foot dry with a towel. Repeat this for the second foot. As you wash the feet, remind each other of the example of Jesus with words. As you wash the first foot say, "I wash your feet in the name of Christ." As you wash the second foot, "As Christ has served us, let us serve one another" or words similar to these. After each person who wishes has participated in washing and being washed, sing or pray in unison an appropriate conclusion such as Richard Gillard's "Servant Song" and Thomas's prayer that follows it. Or use your own ideas for song and prayer.

The Servant Song
> Brother, let me be your servant,
> Let me be as Christ to you.
> Pray that I might have the grace to
> Let you be my servant too.
>
> We are pilgrims on a journey,
> We are brothers on the road;
> We are here to help each other
> Walk the mile and bear the load.
>
> I will hold the Christ-light for you,
> In the night-time of your fear;
> I will hold my hand out for you,
> Speak the peace you long to hear.
>
> I will weep when you are weeping,
> When you laugh I'll laugh with you;
> I will share your joy and sorrow
> Till we've seen this journey through.
>
> When we sing to God in Heaven,
> We shall find such harmony;
> Born of all we've known together
> Of Christ's love and agony.
>
> Sister, let me be your servant,
> Let me be as Christ to you;
> Pray that I might have the grace to
> Let you be my servant too.

FROM THE PRAYERS OF THOMAS À KEMPIS
The Imitation of Christ 3.3

    O Lord my God, you are my total good; who am I, to dare speak to you? I am the least, the poorest of your servants, nothing but a wretched little worm, far poorer and more insignificant than I know or have the courage to say. Yet remember, Lord, that I am nothing, possess nothing, can do nothing. You alone are good, just and holy. You can do all things, grant all things, fill all things, leaving none but the sinner empty of your bounty. Remember your mercies; fill my heart with your grace, for it is not your wish that any of your works should be empty.

    How can I bear this my life of sorrow, if you do not support me with your mercy and grace? Do not turn your face away from me; do not be long in coming to me; do not withdraw your consolation from me, or my soul will become like a land parched with drought. Lord, teach me to do what you want me to do. Teach me to live humbly and worthily in your presence. You are my wisdom; you know me as I really am, as you have done before the world was made, before by birth I came into this world.

IV

THE PATH OF
SUFFERING

Matthew 10:1-33

*C*ome to Jesus. He will help you with your troubles. He will heal your pain. The Christian life is a happy life." It's a common invitation—either by word or by implication. And there is much truth to it. Christian moral behavior prevents a lot of troubles before they start. As for pain, Christ's love cushions it, as does the loving care of his people. And the Christian life has a kind of joy that stands apart from circumstances.

But this kindly invitation to Christian faith is not the full story. People who follow Jesus should expect to suffer. Jesus said so—and Thomas à Kempis echoed it. We suffer because we live in a fallen world where (as bumper stickers proudly declare) "@^#* happens." We suffer because we do stupid, self-ish, sinful things. And in a spiritually hostile environment, we may suffer (as did the disciples) because of our commitment to Christ.

In the grand scheme of events, my own suffering has been small. Indeed, God has given me many pleasures: a home, chil-dren, an able mind, an education, a reliable car, enough money to pay the bills, friends, a wonderful church, a long-term marriage, a willow tree that I love, parents who love me, an early faith in God, enjoyable work, a deepening knowledge of God. And I am truly thankful for these gifts.

But God has also allowed suffering to infiltrate this cozy list of gifts: fractured family relationships that resist all mending, much-loved people who have abandoned their faith, a sister who is mentally ill, a daughter and unborn grandchild killed in a car wreck just weeks after college graduation, and a (well-concealed) rather morose personality that sees a thundercloud behind every rainbow.

Rarely have I suffered for my faith. Yet the path of suffering is part of what it means to follow Jesus; we should expect it. But we can walk with hope because Jesus has walked that path ahead of us.

 ## THE GOOD WORK OF PAIN

THE IMITATION OF CHRIST 1.12, 3.30, 2.12

It's good for you to go through difficult times now and again, and to have your will thwarted; the effect is often to make a man think—make him realize that he is living in exile, and it is no use relying upon any earthly support. It's good for you sometimes to hear men's voices raised against you, and to find that you are making a bad impression, or at least a false impression, on others, even when you are doing your best, and with the best intentions. It often makes for humility; prevents you from having too good an opinion of yourself. It's when we make a bad surface impression, and people are ready to think ill of us, that we learn to fall back upon God's judgments, because he witnesses all our actions from within.

And that is what we are aiming at; a man ought to rely so firmly on God that he has no need to be always looking about for human support. . . .

But now, when the storm is over and you can breathe freely again, recoup your strength in the light of my mercies; for I am near, I the Lord, to restore all things not only to their former perfection, but to pile them high and make them overflow with added graces.

How should any task be too difficult for me? Shall I be like a man who promises something and then fails to do it? Where is your faith? Stand firm and hold your ground. Be a man of courage, and wait in patience; my comfort will come to you in its own good time. Watch out for me; yes, watch; I will come and look after you. The trouble that now distresses you is my way of testing you; the fears which fill you with terror have no foundation. What use is it to worry about what the future will bring? . . . Trust in me, and have confidence in my mercy. Often, when you feel you are far away from me, I am nearer than you think; when you reckon everything is all but lost, a greater reward for your striving is often just ahead of you. Everything is not lost, just because things are going against you. So don't let your present feelings affect your judgment; and don't cling obstinately to any mood of depression, whatever its origin, letting it settle as though you had lost all hope of ever coming out of it.

Don't imagine you have been completely abandoned if I send some trial to afflict you for a while, or if I withdraw from you the comfort you had hoped for; this is the road by which you reach the kingdom of heaven. You may be sure that it is better for you and the rest of my servants to be harassed with things that go against the grain than always to have everything to your liking. I know the thoughts you keep hidden; it is very necessary for your salvation for you to be left now and then without any taste of spiritual sweetness; otherwise, you might start getting conceited ideas about your good progress in the ways of the spirit, and be highly pleased with yourself for reaching a state which is not yet yours. What I have given, I can take away, and restore again when it pleases me to do so.

When I give you something, it is still mine; when I take it back, I am not taking anything of yours, because every good gift, every perfect gift, belongs to me. If I send you some affliction or trouble, do not be indignant about it or let it break your heart; I can quickly relieve you of your burden and turn it all into joy. Nevertheless, I am just, and when I so deal with you, you ought to give me all the praise that is my due. . . .

If there had been anything better for men, more profitable for their salvation, than suffering, you may be sure that Christ, by his teaching and by his own example, would have pointed it out. But no; addressing the disciples who were following him, and all those who wish to follow him, he clearly urges them to carry the cross, when he says: If any man has a mind to come my way, let him renounce self, and take up his cross, and follow me. So then, when we have made an end of reading and studying, this is the conclusion we should reach at last: that we cannot enter the kingdom of heaven without many trials.

 GROUP DISCUSSION OR PERSONAL REFLECTION ——

1. If you were facing a time of suffering, what would be your reaction to this section of *The Imitation of Christ?*

2. What good is suffering—according to Thomas?

3. In paragraphs three through five, Thomas draws on Scripture as he speaks for God. According to this section of his writing, how are we to cope with suffering?

4. "If there had been anything better for men, more profitable for their salvation, than suffering, you may be sure that Christ, by his teaching and by his own example, would have pointed it out. But no. . . . He clearly urges them to carry the cross." When have you seen suffering bring health to a soul, your own or someone else's?

 INTO THE WORD ——————————————————————

5. *Read Matthew 10:1-33.* What instructions did Jesus give his twelve apostles (vv. 1-16)?

6. What suffering did he tell them to expect (vv. 17-25)?

7. What would you find difficult about this assignment?

8. Twice Jesus said, "Do not be afraid," but once he said, "Be afraid." According to Jesus, what is appropriate and what is inappropriate fear during suffering? Why?

9. In one translation of paragraph four above, Thomas speaks of "a vague dread that makes you fear." How might Jesus' words in verses 26-33 help you cope with that kind of fear?

10. Thomas opens this section by saying that suffering causes us to see ourselves as exiles on this earth. Jesus speaks of acknowledging us before his Father in heaven (v. 32). If you are able to see heaven as your true home, how does that help you in some of the current situations that bring you pain?

11. After Jesus had warned his disciples of the suffering they could expect, he said, "It is enough for the student to be like his teacher, and the servant like his master" (v. 25), perhaps foretelling his own suffering. How can you imitate Jesus in your own times of pain?

 ALONG THE ROAD ─────────────────────

❧ Earthliving is hard. When Thomas à Kempis invites us to imitate Jesus, he warns that this will lead down a path of suffering. When Jesus sent his disciples out on a mission, he warned them of the same. Bring to mind some of the suffering that has entered your life. Close your eyes and, in the company of Jesus, gently re-enter that place and time. Share with him, in prayer, the pain you experience, remembering that he also suffered—for you. After a time of prayer, meditate on this line from Thomas: "If there had been anything better for men, more profitable for their salvation than suffering, you may be sure that Christ, by his teaching and by his own example, would have pointed it out. But no." Pray again, asking Jesus to use this suffering to bring health to your soul.

❧ According to Thomas, God says to us, "When I give you something, it is still mine; when I take it back, I am not taking anything of yours, because every good gift, every perfect gift, belongs to me." Meditate on this statement. List some of the gifts (opportunities, skills, people, belongings, inner strengths) that God has given you.

Thank God for these gifts and consider ways that you can enjoy them even more than you do now—because they come directly from God's hand to you. Next consider the potential of loss in this statement from Thomas. As much as you are able, release each gift one by one to God, admitting that it belongs first of all to him. Trust him with the results.

✎ The prayer below from Thomas à Kempis contains the words, "Soak my heart with the rain of heaven." Use the prayer as your own appeal to become soft and pliable in the hands of God.

FROM THE PRAYERS OF THOMAS À KEMPIS
The Imitation of Christ 3.23

O good Jesus, let the brightness of your inward light shine clearly within my mind; banish all darkness from the house of my heart. . . . Send forth your light and your truth to shine upon the earth; I myself am but earth, empty and waste, until you shed your light upon me. Pour down your grace from above; soak my heart with the rain of heaven; bring me streams of devotion to water the face of this earth, to make it bear good and perfect fruit. Take from my mind the load of sin that weighs so heavily upon it, and fix all my desires upon the things of heaven, so that, once I have tasted the sweetness of that joy above, I may be loath to let my thoughts dwell on the things of earth.

Catch hold of me and drag me away from the comfort to be found in things created, a comfort that cannot last; for there is nothing in all creation that can fully slake my longings, fully give me comfort. Bind me to you with a bond of love that cannot be broken; for you alone are all in all for a loving heart, and without you everything else is but pitiful trash.

V

THE PATH OF PEACE
Matthew 7:1-12

A tense hush fell over some four hundred delegates at our denomination's General Assembly. It was Saturday morning, a time when many are zipping suitcases shut and heading for the airport. But the church sanctuary was still crowded. Two of our most respected leaders stood at the front. In careful tones they explained the theological problem, one that has divided Christians for two hundred years. Could our denomination solve it (for us) and stay together? We would find out that morning.

Being Presbyterians, we had formed a committee to study the problem. The chair of the committee named each person who had served with him throughout the two-year period and ordered them to the front. "Stand and face your accusers," he said with mock humor, a prediction they each fervently hoped would not be fulfilled. Then one by one he read the items of their proposed solutions. One by one votes were called and recorded. Shoulders began to relax; smiles began to twitch at the corners of mouths. Minor adjustments to wordings were quickly adopted. The final vote registered not a single "nay." We stood and prayed a prayer of thanks. Peace reigned.

Presbyterians are a contentious lot. We want to get things right—and that triggers disagreement. Already the next knotty theological problem shadows the horizon. Can we solve it with respect and love? Thomas à Kempis and Jesus himself point toward the path of peace.

 CULTIVATING PEACE

THE IMITATION OF CHRIST 2.3

Peace in your own soul first of all, then you can think about making peace between other people. Peaceable folk do more good than learned folk do. When a man is at the mercy of his own feelings, he misinterprets the most innocent actions, always ready to believe the worst; whereas your peaceable man sees good everywhere; at peace in himself, he isn't suspicious of others. It's when you become discontented and unbalanced that your mind is torn by suspicions; there is no rest for you, no rest for those around you. You are always saying the wrong thing, and missing your chance of doing the right thing; you are jealous about your rights, and forget that you have duties. If you will begin by having a high standard yourself, you can afford to have a high standard for other people. How is it that you are so glib in excusing yourself, putting a good color on your own actions, and won't listen when excuses are offered to you? Honesty should make you accuse yourself, excuse your neighbor; bear with him, when you expect him to bear so much from you. Believe me, you've got a long way to go before you can lay claim to real charity, real humility. There should be only one target for all this angry resentment—yourself.

You get on well with gentle, good-natured folk? Why so does everybody; we all like to have friends around us, we all have a soft spot for the man who agrees with us. But when people are difficult and cross-grained, when they get out of hand and keep on contradicting us, to keep on good terms with *them*—ah, that needs a lot of grace; that's a man's job, and you can't praise it too highly.

People differ so; there are contented people, ready to live contentedly with others; and there are restless people, who give no rest to those around them, a burden to others and a worse burden to themselves; and there are those who restrain their own passions, and do their best to restrain the passions of others. But in this imperfect life, when all's said and done, peace doesn't mean having no enemies, it means being ready to put up with ill-treatment. It's the man who has learnt the craft of suffering who really enjoys peace. He is his own master, and the world lies at his feet; he has Christ for his friend, and heaven for his patrimony.

 GROUP DISCUSSION OR PERSONAL REFLECTION ——

1. In this selection from *Imitation,* Thomas à Kempis interweaves descriptions of the person who walks the path of peace with descriptions of people who are not at peace. How does Thomas describe a person of peace? (Find all that you can.)

2. According to Thomas, what are the signs of a person who is not at peace?

3. Which of your own qualities do you see in each description?

4. Thomas mentions several actions that lead to the path of peace. Study each of these. What do you find here that is spiritually wise?

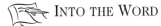 INTO THE WORD ————————————————————

5. *Read Matthew 7:1-12.* Describe the kind of person who lives by the principles Jesus speaks of here.

6. How might the warnings of verses 1-5 help lead to peace between people?

7. Focus on verses 7-12. What all does Jesus reveal about his Father in these verses?

8. How might relating to God in the way that is described here lead to peace?

9. Meditate on verse 12. Why is this command so important?

10. What forces drive peace from your being?

11. Bring to mind one relationship in your life that is not at peace. What do you find in Matthew 7:1-12 that could point you toward the path of peace in that relationship?

12. Thomas à Kempis instructs us to start with "peace in your own soul first of all." In view of all that you have studied here, how could we begin to do that?

 ALONG THE ROAD ──────────────────────────

✐ Thomas à Kempis gives several instructions in the excerpt for this session. Select one statement below that seems particularly appropriate in your own search for peace.

Peace in your own soul first of all, then you can think about making peace with other people.

When a man is at the mercy of his own feelings, he misinterprets the most innocent actions.

Honesty should make you accuse yourself, excuse your neighbor; bear with him.

When people are difficult and cross-grained . . . to keep on good terms with them—ah, that needs a lot of grace . . . and you can't praise it too highly.

In this imperfect life . . . peace doesn't mean having no enemies, it means being ready to put up with ill-treatment.

Meditate for a few minutes on this instruction. What seems wise about it?

Consider how you could begin to do what it suggests. Open your heart to God in prayer asking his help in seeing how (or if) you should begin work in this area. Journal your ideas, concerns or intentions. In one week, look back at your journal writing and add notes about your progress in this area.

Jesus said, "Blessed are the peacemakers, for they shall be called children of God" (NRSV). Thomas à Kempis wrote, "It's the man who has learnt the craft of suffering who really enjoys peace. He is his own master, and the world lies at his feet; he has Christ for his friend, and heaven for his patrimony." Write a letter of peace. This might be addressed to a person (living or dead), an organization or even a nation. Draw on the path of peace as you see it in Jesus' Sermon on the Mount and in the works of Thomas à Kempis. After your letter is complete, pray over it for several days. If it is appropriate, send your letter—along with your prayers for peace.

Spend a week looking for opportunities to make peace. Try to find one each day—even if it is interior peace within yourself. Use that time to invite peace with God. Make a note each day of your encounters.

🖑 Jesus said, "Do not judge, or you too will be judged." Yet judging comes naturally to us, is even sometimes a necessary responsibility. Even then we must remember that we judge through flawed eyes. Bring to mind a person you have judged, perhaps more strenuously than you ought. In prayer, release the person from your judgment.

FROM THE PRAYERS OF THOMAS À KEMPIS
The Imitation of Christ 3.46

The Learner: Lord God, you who as a judge are just, patient and strong, you who know the frailty and crookedness of men, I ask you to be my strength, that I may put complete trust in you; my conscience by itself is not enough. You know what I do not; that should have made me humble myself whenever I was reprimanded, made me meekly bear the reproof. Be merciful; forgive me for all the times I have failed to act in that way; give me grace once more to endure things for longer than I have. The flood of your mercy will better avail me if I would be pardoned, than my protestation of innocence be echoed by my inmost conscience. I may not be conscious of any fault, but that is no reason for complacency; if you withhold your mercy, what man is there living that can stand guiltless in your presence?

VI

Following to the End

John 11:1-44

Sanna, strong and beautiful in the best tradition of her Nordic ancestors, was wife to a physician and mother to three equally beautiful young daughters. She wrote exquisite poetry, crafted whimsical children's books, taught creative writing at a nearby college, and dressed her home with wildflowers, antiques and natural light. A favorite sailing photo captures her energy, with the sun on her face and the wind in her hair as if all the world lay before her—ready for her enjoyment. But Sanna was dying.

Near the end, she asked to speak to our church congregation one more time. Now frail and quivering, she spoke with a croaking voice the words she had memorized in childhood.

What is your only comfort, in life and in death?

That I belong—body and soul, in life and in death—not to myself but to my faithful Savior, Jesus Christ.[1]

---

[1] Heidelberg Catechism, Question 1, 1563.

Sanna went on to explain what those words meant to her (and to us) when death comes far sooner than expected. She committed her children to our care and herself to the care of God. And as tears welled in our eyes, she comforted us.

Sometimes the best preparation for life is a preparation for death.

 ## Living to Die

The Imitation of Christ 1.23

Your time here is short, very short; take another look at the way in which you spend it. Here man is today; tomorrow, he is lost to view; and once a man is out of sight, it's not long before he passes out of mind. How dull they are, how obdurate, these hearts of ours, always occupied with the present, instead of looking ahead to what lies before us! Every action of yours, every thought, should be those of a man who expects to die before the day is out. Death would have no great terrors for you if you had a quiet conscience, would it? Then why not keep clear of sin, instead of running away from death? If you aren't fit to face death today, it's very unlikely you will be by tomorrow; besides, tomorrow is an uncertain quantity; you have no guarantee that there will be any tomorrow—for you.

What's the use of having a long life, if there's so little improvement to show for it? Improvement? Unfortunately it happens, only too often, that the longer we live the more we add to our guilt. If only we could point to one day in our life here that was really well spent! Years have passed by since we turned to God; and how little can we show, many of us, in the way of solid results! Fear death if you will, but don't forget that long life may have greater dangers for you.

Well for you, if you keep an eye on your deathbed all the time, and put yourself in the right dispositions for death as each day passes. Perhaps, before now, you've seen a man die? Remember, then, that you have got the same road to travel.

Each morning, imagine to yourself that you won't last till evening; and when night comes, don't make bold to promise yourself a new day. Be ready for it all the time; so live, that death cannot take you unawares.

Plenty of people die quite suddenly, without any warning; the Son of Man will appear just when we are not expecting him. And when that last hour comes, you'll find yourself taking a completely different view of the life that lies behind you. How bitterly you will regret all that carelessness, all that slackening of effort!

If you hope to live well and wisely, try to be, here and now, the man you would want to be on your deathbed. What will give you confidence then—the confidence which ensures a happy death? . . .

Sometime, you'll know what it is to wish you had another day, even another hour, to put your life straight; and will you get it? There's no saying.

My friend, my very dear friend, only think what dangers you can avoid, what anxieties you can escape, if you will be anxious *now*, sensitive *now* to the thought of death! Make it your business so to live, today, that you can meet death with a smile, not with a shudder, when it comes. . . .

Live in this world like some stranger from abroad, dismissing its affairs as no concern of yours; keep your heart free, and trained up toward God in heaven—you have no lasting citizenship here. Heaven must be the home you long for daily, with prayers and sighs and tears, if your soul, after death, is to find a happy passage to its Master's presence.

 GROUP DISCUSSION OR PERSONAL REFLECTION——

1. How might Sanna's quotation from the Heidelberg Confession help you to *live?*

2. Do you find this section from *The Imitation of Christ* helpful or troubling? Explain.

3. Thomas says that we are to try to be "here and now" the person "you would want to be on your deathbed." If you were to do this, what preparations would you want to make?

  INTO THE WORD ─────────────────────

4. *Read John 11:1-44.* Put yourself in the shoes of each character in the story. As one of the disciples, what do you learn about Jesus?

as Mary?

as Martha?

as Lazarus?

5. What have these characters learned about life and about death?

6. Focus on verses 25-26. How would you explain Jesus' description of himself to someone unfamiliar with the Christian faith?

7. How do you answer the question Jesus asked? Explain.

8. How does your answer to Jesus' question impact your thoughts about life and death?

9. Lazarus had to die again—later. What impact do you think the events of this chapter would have on the way he approached his second death?

10. Jesus himself was about to die. What comfort might these three friends from Bethany find in their memories of what happened there?

11. How might this account of Jesus and his three friends encourage you to follow Jesus to the end?

12. Read again Sanna's question and answer from the Heidelberg Confession. How might this statement bring comfort in the current circumstances of your life?

13. How might it help you to cope with death—your own or the death of someone you love?

 ALONG THE ROAD ————————————————

Thomas à Kempis wrote, "Live in this world like some stranger from abroad, dismissing its affairs as no concern of yours." If you were to do this, how would your status as a pilgrim and stranger here impact various areas of your life? Consider your

work or study

belongings

relationships with Christians

relationships with unbelievers

ways of dealing with disappointment

relationship with God

Meditate on what it means to be a pilgrim and stranger on earth with heaven as your home. Then focus on one or more of the items listed above, addressing them as a pilgrim whose true home is in heaven. In prayer, ask God's help as you live and act accordingly.

✐ Consider the full text answering the first question of the Heidelberg Catechism.

What is your only comfort in life and in death?

That I belong—body and soul, in life and in death—not to myself but to my faithful Savior, Jesus Christ, who at the cost of his own blood has fully paid for all my sins and has completely freed me from the dominion of the devil; that he protects me so well that without the will of my Father in heaven not a hair can fall from my head; indeed, that everything must fit his purpose for my salvation. Therefore, by his Holy Spirit, he also assures me of eternal life, and makes me wholeheartedly willing and ready from now on to live for him.

Carefully consider each phrase of this statement, making notes as you go along. Notice that the statement speaks of both life and death. (Sometimes life is harder than death.) After your study, write a prayer of response to God.

✐ Prayerfully read Jesus' words to grieving Martha in John 11:25-26. Hear him speak those words to you as well. Circle phrases that seem particularly important and think carefully of their implications. Bring to Jesus your fears about life and about death and eternity. Bring to him your sense of alienation in a world that is far from perfect. Allow his words to fill you with hope. As you answer his question at the end, pray your own commitment to him in response.

✐ Bring to mind someone who is experiencing loss. (This might be through illness, death, job loss, divorce, disappointment or other difficulties.) Find a way this week to share the comfort you have received through this chapter.

FROM THE PRAYERS OF THOMAS À KEMPIS

The Imitation of Christ 3.57

Bless you, Lord, for those words of yours! They taste sweeter in my mouth than honey and the honeycomb. Whatever should I do in trials and troubles as great as mine are, if I hadn't the support of your holy words? If only I get to the safety of heaven's harbor at last, what do I care what I go through, or how much? Let my ending be a good one, Lord, my passing from this world a happy one. Keep me in mind, O my God, and guide me straight to your kingdom. Amen.

How to Lead a Christian Classics Bible Study

If you are leading a small group discussion using this series, we have good news for you: you do not need to be an expert on Christian history. We have provided the information you need about the historical background in the introduction to each study. Reading more of the original work of these writers will be helpful but is not necessary. We have set each reading in context within the introductions to each study. Further background and helps are found in the study notes to each session as well. And a bibliography is provided at the end of each guide.

In leading the Bible study portion of each study you will be helped by a resource like *Leading Bible Discussions* in our LifeGuide® Bible Study series as well as books dealing with small group dynamics like *The Big Book on Small Groups*. But, once again, you do not need to be an expert on the Bible. The Bible studies are designed to follow the flow of the passage from observation to interpretation to application. You may feel that the studies lead themselves! The study notes at the back will help you through the tough spots.

What Is Your Job as a Leader?

☐ To pray that God will be at work in your heart and mind as well as in the hearts and minds of the group members.

☐ To thoroughly read all of the studies, Scripture texts and all of the helps in this guide before the study.

☐ To help people to feel comfortable as they arrive and to encourage everyone to participate in the discussion.

☐ To encourage group members to apply what they are learning in the study session and by using the "Along the Road" sections between sessions.

Study Notes

Study One. Following Jesus. Matthew 4:18-22; 8:18-27.
Purpose: To imitate the teachings and life of Jesus.

Question 1. In recent years, WWJD bracelets, ribbons and key rings have appeared throughout the Christian subculture. They remind the wearer (or carrier) to stop and think: "What would Jesus do?" But answers are not easy. Jesus didn't walk in our culture. Many of the decisions we make just aren't treated in biblical texts. What would Jesus do if his teenagers stayed out all night? Or if the sales manager said, "Meet this quota next month or else"? Or if the student Christian leaders' retreat is all of next week, but if you don't work that week you might have trouble paying next term's tuition? Thomas removes us one step from the question of "What would Jesus do?" and points us instead to principles. In the opening paragraph, he invites us to follow Jesus in "his teachings and his manner of living." As you work with this question, think of what you know of the teachings of Jesus and of the way that he lived. Then respond as you are able.

Question 3. Consider how this might impact your praying, the way you choose to obey (or not obey) certain biblical principles and your own expectations of God's work on your behalf.

Question 4. Notice the personal nature of Jesus' call and his description of that call.

Question 6. Jesus' conversation with these two people show such high demands for following him that we are tempted to think that surely Jesus did not mean what he said. We wonder what is written between the lines.

Perhaps not much. Discipleship was costly—then as now. It is possible, however, that the young man wishing to "bury his father" may have had a long wait in view. His father may not yet have been near death and the young man may have simply wanted to wait for many years until his father died so that he could collect his inheritance. Jesus' statement "Let the dead bury their own dead" may have pointed to the spiritual death of those who did not believe in him. In that case, those who are spiritually dead (not his followers) could take care of the burial on the son's behalf. We know from later events that Jesus did not lack compassion at a time of death. He wept at the tomb of Lazarus, and he committed his mother to the care of John at his own death. Even so, we can see from the two conversations recorded in Matthew 8 that following Jesus was costly business.

Question 7. A follow-up question might be, "What should a person following Jesus be prepared for?"

Question 10. Consider what Jesus' sleep, his rebuke to the disciples, then his impact on the storm reveals about him. What could the disciples (and we) begin to understand about his nature?

Question 11. Explore what you know of Jesus from Scripture, but also what you have learned about Jesus from your experience as one of his followers.

Along the Road. If you are meeting with a group, consider providing time for quiet work on one or more of these questions, then come together to share your insights. Some groups devote an entire second session to extended work on this section, spending time in writing, meditation, prayer and conversation.

Study Two. The Path of Grace. Matthew 5:1-12.
Purpose: To grow toward Christ's image by developing a character based on grace.

Question 1. Before analyzing this rather complex passage from Thomas à Kempis, try to gather a general impression based on a first reading. Do you feel positive or negative about it? Why? Would you want to know a person whose character was based on grace? to have that person as a friend? Why, or why not? Do you see ingredients of yourself in these descriptions? How so? What is your response to the last paragraph?

Question 2. If you are working with a group, allow time for people to create the visual contrast of character qualities outlined in the question. Then consider how the qualities of grace might, or might not, be accepted in your culture. Consider also how they might be perceived in your church or student group.

Question 3. Take a third look at this passage from Thomas à Kempis. Where do you see yourself in the life of grace? What areas do you find challenging? Would you want to move in that direction? Why or why not?

Question 6. We tend to think of mourning as personal grief over a death of someone we love. Jesus comforts and blesses those in that kind of grief. But the Beatitude about mourning probably goes beyond that kind of grief. Scripture is full of godly people who mourned over sin, not necessarily their own sins, but the sins of their people. (See the prayer of Moses in Ex 32:30-34, the prayer of Solomon as he anticipated sin even as he dedicated the temple in 2 Chron 6:14-42, and the prayer of Ezra as he confessed the sins of his people in Ezra 9:5-15.) As you reflect on the groups you belong to (nation, church, school, family), consider your own responsibility within those groups. The people of a church, for example, are so much a single unit that Scripture calls the church by a single name, "the body of Christ" (1 Cor 12:27). Here the sins of one are in some sense the responsibility of all, and mourning over sin is appropriate. What brings you to mourning? What is an appropriate way to express that grief?

Question 7. Refer to the introduction to this chapter for one example of meekness. You may have met similar people. If so, thank God for them. For further reflection consider: Why would Jesus say that such people "inherit the earth"? How can you imitate Christ in the ways that he was meek?

Question 8. If you are in a group, allow a few moments for people to silently consider the implications of these terms. They may want to share those reflections and then consider together the hope offered in this verse.

New Bible Dictionary (Downers Grove, Ill: InterVarsity Press, 1962) defines *righteousness* in several ways. First, it is a right relationship between God and a person, and also between a person and all other people. Righteousness also speaks of God's gracious actions toward his own people. In addition, God himself is righteous as Creator, Redeemer, Savior and Judge. Righteousness can also refer to the actions of people when they conform to the demands and obligations of the will of God. But righteousness is also a gift given by God to those he has redeemed. In summary, "The gift of God's righteousness involves entry into the new realm of divine salvation, the gift of eternal life under the reign of God. . . . Hence the extrinsic righteousness imputed through the cross finds inevitable expression in the intrinsic righteousness of a life which in a new way conforms to the will of God, even though the ultimate realization of this conformity must await the consummation of the kingdom." Clearly, the term *righteousness* covers a lot of territory. Those who are filled with righteousness are greatly blessed indeed.

Question 9. We are all deeply flawed people. As we recognize our own sin, we receive with thanksgiving God's mercy toward us. Having received from him a mercy we do not deserve, we can hardly withhold a similar mercy from others. "Blessed are the merciful for they will be shown mercy" probably refers first to the mercy God grants to us, but also the circle of mercy created among his people when undeserved mercy shown to one person inspires a return of similar mercy. Mercy is the only way for flawed humans to live in kindness toward each other.

Question 11. After you have surveyed your opportunities to make peace, consider where and how you can best focus your peacemaking efforts.

Question 12. Be sure to look at both the warning and the encouragement in these verses. We might think that people who cultivate the character qualities described in the first seven "blesseds" would live a life of peace and prosperity. Jesus says that this is not to be expected. Instead we should expect persecution—and that too is blessed. He then provides various forms of encouragement as he closes this section of his Sermon on the Mount.

Along the Road. If you are meeting with a group, consider using this section in a separate session or at the close of your meeting. Provide time for personal study and prayer, then discuss your insights and your intentions for the coming week. When you come to the names listed next to the Beatitudes, listen to each other's stories of people they have known who live by these principles. Thank God together for them. Pray for each other as you take on the assignment for the week ahead. Then, when you gather again, ask how God has used your individual efforts to imitate the character of Christ.

Study Three. The Path of Humility. John 13:1-17.
Purpose: To practice humility in our relationships with God and with each other.

Question 2. Thomas deals with both aspects of judging (judging others and judging ourselves) in the first two paragraphs of this text. Notice the dangers and difficulties of both kinds of judgment. Consider particularly our natural bent toward self-protection when we judge ourselves.

Question 4. Spend some time meditating on this profound statement from Thomas à Kempis. Consider the dangers of self-love. Consider the losing and finding mentioned here. Consider what it means to find ourselves—in the way that Thomas describes. Consider how is that different from self-love? Reflect on a personal experience or stage of spiritual development that has verified (or conflicted) with this statement. If you want to "buy in to" what Thomas says here, what shifts might that make in your thoughts and actions? If you are discussing this study with a group, consider pausing here and (after time for personal reflection) discussing some of the questions above. If your group spends an extra session working through "Along the Road," you can move this question to that section and discuss it then.

Question 5. Try to see this event through several characters present: Peter, Judas, Jesus, other observers.

Question 6. Look through the whole passage citing ways that Jesus reveals his love.

Question 7. Verse 3 gives an unusual picture of Jesus' self-knowledge. Use this picture as you try to blend it with his actions of the evening. Why would a person with this kind of knowledge about his or her power—past and future—take on the role described at this table? What does that mean about our own observations of status with each other?

Question 8. Examine the shifts in Peter's thinking during the course of this dialogue. What is the undercurrent of symbolism in the various kinds of washing they discussed? Why did Peter not want his feet washed? Why didn't Jesus wash all of him as he asked?

Along the Road. If you are doing this section with a group, open your time with a discussion of question 4. Then allow time for people to write the prayer described in the first activity. Encourage any who wish to read their prayers aloud during a time of shared prayer together. Consider washing each other's feet as described here, then end by singing together "The Servant Song" and reading aloud the prayer from Thomas à Kempis. If you are using this section privately, prayerfully consider the concepts here. Create journal notes, prayers and songs in your worship of God.

Study Four. The Path of Suffering. Matthew 10:1-33.

Purpose: To expect suffering and invite God to use the hardships of our lives to nourish our souls.

Question 1. Thomas invites a strenuous spirituality. Be honest with yourself as you place your own suffering beside what he describes.

Question 2. Paragraphs one, two and seven focus on the ways God sometimes uses suffering for good, but other paragraphs touch on it as well.

Question 4. If you are in a group, use this question to share your observations of the relationship between suffering and spiritual growth. Take caution, however, that you do not try to find a reason behind various painful events. We should not expect to find answers to many of the "why questions" that surround suffering. We can expect that God's reasons are hidden in his mystery. Instead, focus on the character of God, the "who questions," who God is. Then notice how God uses suffering to work within the soul and draw us into his image. Follow-up questions might be: How are you spiritually different because of this painful event? What spiritual differences do you see in (insert name) after this period of suffering?

Question 5. These sixteen verses are full of instructions. Find all that you can.

Question 8. We tend to fear physical suffering much more than the spiritual. Yet Jesus says here that even death is not a valid fear. And he reassures us that physical things even as small as one of our hairs or even a fallen sparrow are not beyond his attention. But he warns us to fear "the One who can destroy both soul and body in hell" (v. 28). This relates to his challenge to persevere in faith even when it is hardest to keep on believing—to acknowledge him even in the face of suffering (vv. 32-33).

Question 11. What did Jesus mean when he said, "It is enough for a student to be like his teacher"? Verse 25 has several possible interpretations. It may mean that the followers of Jesus should expect to suffer; he did (Davidson). It may also be a more general command that we as Christ's followers are to model him in all possible ways (Calvin). We should also notice the warning in the second half of this verse. Satan also has his followers, people who imitate him. We should guard our actions lest they imitate those in that household.

Study Five. The Path of Peace. Matthew 7:1-12.

Purpose: To create peace between ourselves and other people, as well as between ourselves and God.

Question 1. You will find several descriptions of a person of peace in this section from Thomas à Kempis. According to Thomas, a person of peace makes others feel at peace, is a profit to him or herself, to others and so on. If you are in a group, save the longer list of what a person of peace *is not* for the next question.

Question 2. A person who is not at peace turns good into evil, believes the worst, is suspicious and so on. Thorough answers to these first two questions will help you personalize the next one.

Question 4. For a quick summary of the actions Thomas à Kempis advises, see the five quotations in "Along the Road."

Question 5. You will find clues to describing a person of peace in almost every verse of this passage. Verse 6 is confusing and seems not to fit with the rest of the passage. *New Bible Commentary* (Downers Grove, Ill.: Inter-Varsity Press, 1994) helps us sort it out. "Verse 6 indicates that there is also a right kind of judgment which the disciple is called to exercise. . . . Holy and valuable things should be given only to those able to appreciate them. No specific application is indicated, but we may remember that there is a time to speak and a time to be silent (Ec. 3:7). God's truth must not be exposed unnecessarily to abuse and mockery."

Question 8. Much of our discord with people comes because we expect too much from them—and we look to them to fulfill our needs. Jesus invites us to knock, seek, ask—of God. If we turn our expectations toward God instead of people we are less likely to be disappointed. Also verse 12 (the "Golden Rule") guides all of our human relationships toward peace.

Question 9. This verse has often been paraphrased as "The Golden Rule." Jesus himself said that it summed up the "Law and the Prophets." Study its content and try to determine why it merits such lofty descriptions.

Along the Road. Several of these activities can be adapted to group use. If you are doing this section of the study as a group, allow appropriate time for writing and prayer, then join together to share your thoughts. Pray for each other as you try to live out peace in the days ahead.

Study Six. Following to the End. John 11:1-44.
Purpose: To follow Christ, in life and in death, until the end.

Question 1. The opening line of this confession speaks of both life and death. We often focus on the death aspect because of our own fears. Yet life is sometimes more challenging than death. So, during this question, consider how these truths can help you to *live*. You will focus on the death aspect of the statement later in the study.

Question 2. Some of Thomas's statements are troubling; some are helpful. Examine both as you survey his text. Then conclude, overall, which is more powerful for you.

Question 3. Consider practical, spiritual and relational preparations.

Question 4. Think about this question *before* you read the text. As you read try to see the events and conversations through the eyes of one or more of the characters. After you have studied the perspective of one person, shift to another. (They each encountered Jesus differently and would have learned different things about him.) Use this technique as you work with question 5. If you are working with a group, assign a different character for each of the two questions to a different person. Then compile your findings so that your group gains a multi-perspective view of Jesus and his teachings as revealed throughout the entire passage.

Question 6. Use this question to examine your own beliefs about this statement—as well as how you might explain it to others. Explain who Jesus is and then explain such concepts as "resurrection," "life," "belief," "never die." Martha's answer in verse 27 may help.

Question 8. If we believe all that Jesus said about himself in verse 25, this will have a profound effect on all that we think and do. For example:

How would this belief impact your choice of work?

How would it impact how you feel when waiting for the results of medical tests?

How would it impact what you do with your money?

How would it impact your relationships with other Christians?

How would it impact the priorities you set for your family?

Along the Road. Use this section for your own spiritual development as you communicate with God and share what he has given you with people whose lives you touch. If you are meeting with a group, adapt this section for group use by allowing time for meditation, writing and personal prayer. Then come together to share your findings and to discuss your plans for putting them into practice. Consider reading your prayers as a part of your prayer time together.

Sources

Study One
Thomas à Kempis, *The Imitation of Christ,* trans. Ronald Knox and Michael Oakley (South Bend, Ind.: Greenlawn, 1990), pp. 3, 71, 90-92. *Imitation of Christ,* pp. 218-19.

Study Two
Imitation of Christ, pp. 169-73.

Study Three
Imitation of Christ, pp. 21-22, 94-95.

Study Four
Imitation of Christ, pp. 17, 119-20, 128-30.

Study Five
Imitation of Christ, pp. 57-58, 153-54.

Study Six
Imitation of Christ, pp. 38-41, 178.

Further Reading

Bechtel, Paul A., ed. *The Imitation of Christ: Thomas à Kempis*. Chicago: Moody Press, 1980.

Cruise, F. R. *Thomas à Kempis: Notes of a Visit to the Scenes in Which His Life Was Spent, with Some Account of the Examination of His Relics*. London: K. Paul, Trench, Trübner, 1887.

De Montmorency, J. E. G. *Thomas à Kempis: His Age and Book*. London: Methuen, 1906.

Elwell, Walter A. "Religion's Second-Best Seller." *Christianity Today*, September 3, 1982, pp. 33-34.

Gardiner, Harold C., S.J. *The Imitation of Christ: Thomas à Kempis*. Garden City, N.Y.: Doubleday, 1976.

Griffin, William, trans. *The Imitation of Christ: How Jesus Wants Us to Live*. New York: HarperCollins, 2001.

Ives, Eben. J. *The Message of Thomas à Kempis*. London: Student Christian Movement, 1922.

Knox, Ronald, and Michael Oakley, trans. *The Imitation of Christ by Thomas à Kempis*. South Bend, Ind.: Greenlawn Press, 1990.

Shahar, Shulamith. *Childhood in the Middle Ages*. Translated by Chaya Galai. New York: Routledge, 1990.

Thomas à Kempis. *The Chronicles of the Canons Regular of Mount St. Agnes*. London: K. Paul, Trench, Trubner, 1906.

—————. *The Complete Works of Thomas à Kempis*. London: K. Paul, Trench, Trübner, 1907.

—————. *The Soliloquy of the Soul*, to which has been added meditations and prayers for sick persons by George Stanhope. Hartford: Printed by

John Babcock, 1800. (microform) Early American Imprints, Second Series. Microopaque. New York: Readex Microprint Corporation, 1969.

————. *The Valley of Lilies* and *The Soliloquy of the Soul.* New Bedford, Mass.: Printed and sold by A. Shearman, 1897. (microform) Early American Imprints, Second Series. Microopaque. New York: Readex Microprint Corporation, 1969.

Tuchman, Barbara W. *A Distant Mirror: The Calamitous 14th Century.* New York: Alfred A. Knopf, 1978.

Wesley, John, trans. *The Christian's Pattern: Extracts from The Imitation of Christ by Thomas à Kempis.* Salem, Ohio: Schmul, n.d. Reprinted from Wesley's abridged edition of 1777.

Wyon, Olive. "Devotional and Pastoral Classics: Thomas à Kempis, 'The Imitation of Christ.'" *The Expository Times* 69 (October 1957): 81-83.